Piano Exam Pieces

ABRSM Grade 6

Selected from the 2017 & 2018 syllabus

Name

D1326810

Date of exam

Contents

Editor for ABRSM: Richard Jones

Other pieces for Grade 6

LIST A

4 **J. S. Bach** Andante: 3rd movt from Pastorella in F, BWV 590, trans. Whittaker. P. 16 from *Bach Transcriptions for Piano* (OUP)

5 **Beethoven** Andante: 1st movt from Sonata in G minor, Op. 49 No. 1. Sonata published individually (ABRSM) or Beethoven, *The 35 Piano Sonatas*, Vol. 1 (ABRSM)

6 **D. Scarlatti** Sonata in F, Kp. 378 (L. 276). Scarlatti, *3 Sonatas for Keyboard* (Bärenreiter) or No. 123 from Scarlatti, *200 Sonatas*, Vol. 3 (Editio Musica Budapest)

LIST B

4 **Cervantes** Los tres golpes. *Beyond the Romantic Spirit*, Book 1 (Alfred)

5 **Hummel** Andantino in A flat (No. 57 from *Klavierschule*). No. 8 from Hummel, *16 Short Pieces* (ABRSM)

6 **Martinů** Pohádka (Fairy-Tale): No. 4 from *Loutky*, Book 1 (Bärenreiter) or *Loutky*, Books 1–3 (Bärenreiter)

LIST C

4 **Mike Cornick** Modulations: from *Blue Piano* (Universal) or *Encore*, Book 3 (ABRSM)

5 **Dello Joio** Moderate: 1st movt from Suite for Piano (G. Schirmer) or *20th Century American Composers*, Upper Intermediate Level (G. Schirmer)

6 **Khachaturian** Study: No. 5 from *Pictures of Childhood* (Boosey & Hawkes)

THE MUSIC SHOP £8·25

First published in 2016 by ABRSM (Publishing) Ltd,
a wholly owned subsidiary of ABRSM, 24 Portland Place,
London W1B 1LU, United Kingdom
© 2016 by The Associated Board of the Royal Schools of Music
Distributed worldwide by Oxford University Press

Music origination by Julia Bovee
Cover by Kate Benjamin & Andy Potts
Printed in England by Caligraving Ltd, Thetford,
Norfolk, on materials from sustainable sources.

Invention in A minor

BWV 784

No. 13 of 15 Inventions from *Aufrichtige Anleitung*

J. S. Bach
(1685–1750)

In 1722–3 Bach entered 30 newly composed pieces into the *Clavierbüchlein* (Little Keyboard Book) for his young son Wilhelm Friedemann. The first 15, each entitled 'Praeambulum', were in two contrapuntal parts, and the second 15, each entitled 'Fantasia', in three parts. Shortly afterwards, in early 1723, he wrote out a fair copy of the 30 pieces under the title 'Aufrichtige Anleitung' (Sincere Instruction), bringing them into their definitive form. The two-part pieces were now entitled 'Inventio' (Invention), and the three-part pieces 'Sinfonia'. According to the new title page, the Inventions and Sinfonias were designed to foster good playing in two and three parts, to help students to invent and develop good musical ideas, and above all 'to arrive at a *cantabile* style of playing and acquire a strong foretaste for composition.'

The Invention in A minor, selected here, is built on the principle of imitation between the two hands, first led by the right hand, and later (b. 6) by the left. No less significant in *cantabile* pieces of this kind is the period structure (a period being equivalent to a sentence in language). This piece falls into three periods, each marked by a clear cadence. The first period cadences in C major (key III) at b. 6; the second, in E minor (key v) at b. 13; and the third, in A minor (key i) at the end. Dynamics are left to the player's discretion.

Source: autograph fair copy (1723), Staatsbibliothek zu Berlin, Preußischer Kulturbesitz, Musikabteilung, Mus.ms.Bach P610

Reproduced from J. S. Bach: *Inventions & Sinfonias*, BWV 772–801, edited by Richard Jones (ABRSM)

A:2

Courante

Third movement from Partita in C minor, HWV 444

G. F. Handel
(1685–1759)

The Partita in C minor, from which this Courante is selected, is thought to be one of Handel's earliest keyboard works, perhaps composed around 1705–6 when he was only about 20 and living in the North German city of Hamburg. There he played the violin, and later harpsichord, in the Hamburg opera. At that time, too, he composed keyboard pieces, arias, cantatas, and his first opera *Almira*. The Partita is made up of five movements – Prélude, Allemande, Courante, Gavotte and Menuet. Although the Courante has a French title like the other movements, it is written in the style of an Italian corrente. The word 'corrente' means 'running', so dances of this type are in quick triple time, with evenly flowing semiquavers in the right hand. French courantes, on the other hand, are slower and tend to oscillate between $\frac{3}{2}$ and $\frac{6}{4}$ time.

Editorial square brackets above the stave (⌐⎯⌐) denote hemiola rhythm – two bars of triple time are to be accented as if they were three bars of duple time. Hemiola is very common in Baroque dances, especially in the cadential bars at the end of a phrase. Dynamics are left to the player's discretion. All trill signs are editorial additions.

Source: MS copy, Staatsbibliothek zu Berlin, Preußischer Kulturbesitz, Musikabteilung, Mus.ms. 9164/3

Rondo

Third movement from Sonata in C, K. 545

W. A. Mozart
(1756–91)

The Sonata in C, K. 545, was one of Mozart's last piano sonatas, completed in Vienna on 26 June 1788 – the same day as the great E flat major Symphony, K. 543. The Sonata was written for teaching purposes but it nonetheless represents Mozart at his finest.

Selected here is the finale, which is a simple rondo: A (b. 1, key C), B (b. 8, G), A (b. 20, C), C (b. 28, A minor), A (b. 52, C), coda (b. 60, C). The rondo theme A illustrates Mozart's preoccupation with strict counterpoint at this point in his life – it opens as a canon at the lower 5th. Denis Matthews (ABRSM edition) points out that 'articulation, not speed, gives the movement its vitality' and 'pedalling should be minimal'. Dynamics are left to the player's discretion. Mozart's autograph manuscript has not survived, and the work remained unpublished during his lifetime, so this text is based on the posthumous first edition of 1805.

Source: *Sonate facile pour le pianoforte composée par W. A. Mozart. Oeuvre posthume.* (Vienna: Bureau d'Arts et d'Industrie, 1805)

B:1

Scherzo

No. 2 from *Akvareller*, Op. 19

N. W. Gade
(1817–90)

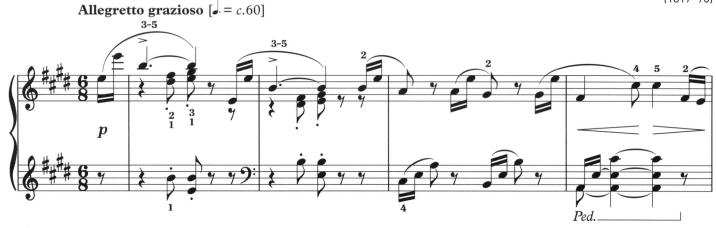

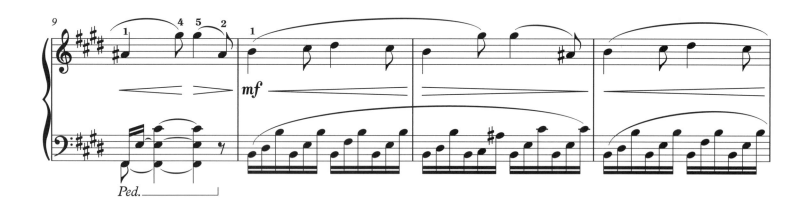

Niels Wilhelm Gade was the outstanding Danish composer before Nielsen. He visited Leipzig in the early 1840s, became friendly with Mendelssohn, and in 1844 was appointed assistant conductor of the Leipzig Gewandhaus Orchestra and teacher at the conservatory. He succeeded Mendelssohn as conductor of the orchestra in 1847, but soon had to return to Denmark due to the outbreak of war. Back home he became director of the Copenhagen Academy of Music in 1849 and, from 1866, joint director of the new Copenhagen Conservatory.

Despite Gade's Scandinavian roots, much of his output is Germanic in style and strongly influenced by Mendelssohn and Schumann. His collection of piano pieces entitled *Akvareller* (Watercolours), dates from 1850. It comprises two volumes, each containing five pieces. The Scherzo selected here is notable for its Mendelssohn-like lightness of touch.

Source: *Aquarelles, Poésies musicales* (Paris: G. Flaxland, *c*.1850)

Slow Waltz

Valse lente

Op. 33

Oskar Merikanto
(1868–1924)

The Finnish composer Oskar Merikanto studied composition in Helsinki, Leipzig and Berlin. After his return to Finland, he was employed as an organist, and from 1911 to 1922 he conducted the Finnish National Opera in Helsinki.

Valse lente dates from 1898. It is written in a Romantic style and in ternary form (ABA[1] + coda), with the middle section B starting in the relative minor at b. 17, the abridged return of A at b. 37, and the coda at b. 45.

Source: *Valse lente*, Op. 33 (Helsinki: K. G. Fazer, n. d.)

B:3

Prelude in E

No. 9 from 24 Preludes, Op. 11

A. N. Skryabin
(1872–1915)

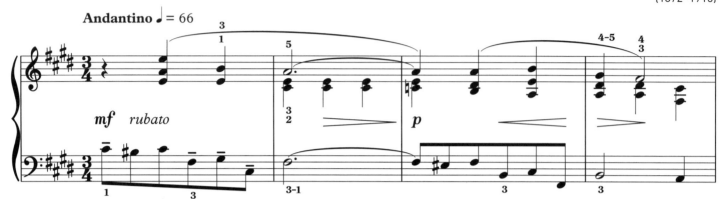

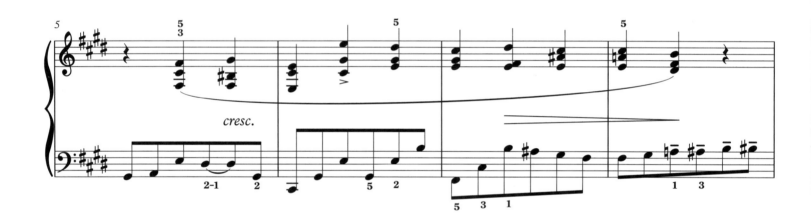

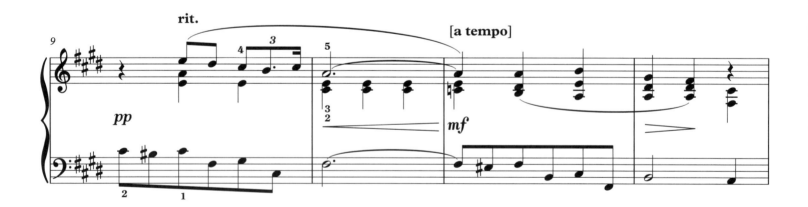

The Russian composer and pianist Aleksandr Nikolayevich Skryabin studied at the Moscow Conservatory from 1888 to 1892, after which he embarked on a successful career as a concert pianist, playing mainly his own music and that of Chopin. He taught at the Moscow Conservatory from 1898 to 1902 and then moved to Western Europe, not returning to Russia till 1909.

Skryabin's 24 Preludes, Op. 11, is one of many sets of preludes and/or fugues that have been influenced by Bach's *Well-Tempered Clavier*. Like Bach's collection, it contains a prelude in every major and minor key. However, whereas Bach orders the keys chromatically, Skryabin orders them according to the circle of 5ths. This corresponds to Chopin's ordering in his 24 Preludes, Op. 28, which is likely to have been Skryabin's immediate model.

Source: first edition, *24 Préludes*, Op. 11 (Leipzig: M. P. Belaieff, 1897)

Stick Dance

Joc cu bâtă

No. 1 from *Román népi táncok*

Béla Bartók
(1881–1945)

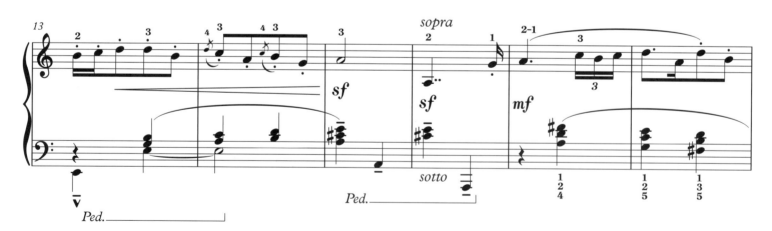

In the first decade of the 20th century, the Hungarian composer Béla Bartók, alongside his compatriot Kodály, began to collect the folksongs of his native land, as well as those of neighbouring Romania. During the First World War, Bartók, a virtuoso pianist, hardly performed at all, but he made many arrangements of folk music. The year 1915 saw the composition of three works based on Romanian tunes: *Román kolinda dallamok* (Romanian Christmas Songs), the Sonatina and *Román népi táncok* (Romanian Folk Dances), from which this piece is selected, and which has become one of Bartók's most popular works. The dances were subsequently arranged by the composer for small orchestra (1917) and by Zoltán Székely for violin and piano (1925–6). Although the composer's metronome mark is ♩ = 100, candidates may prefer a slower tempo, for example ♩ = c.88.

Source: Bartók: *Rumänische Volkstänze* (Universal Edition, 1918)

Cruella de Vil

from *The 101 Dalmations*

Arranged by Pete Churchill

Melville A. Leven
(1914–2007)

The American composer and lyricist Mel Leven had a long association with Walt Disney's company. Of his many songs, perhaps the most famous was 'Cruella de Vil', written for the 1961 Disney film *The 101 Dalmatians* (based on Dodie Smith's 1956 novel of that name). The lyrics begin:

Cruella de Vil, Cruella de Vil,
If she doesn't scare you, no evil thing will,
To see her is to take a sudden chill,
Cruella, Cruella de Vil.

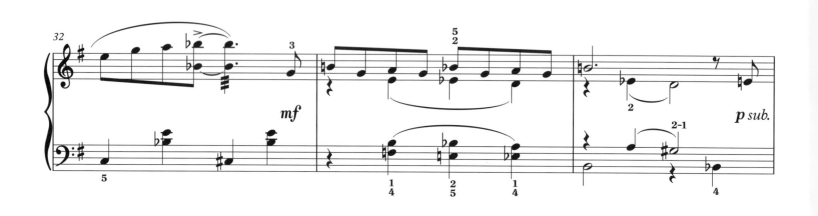

Masquerade

 C:3

Karen Tanaka
(born 1961)

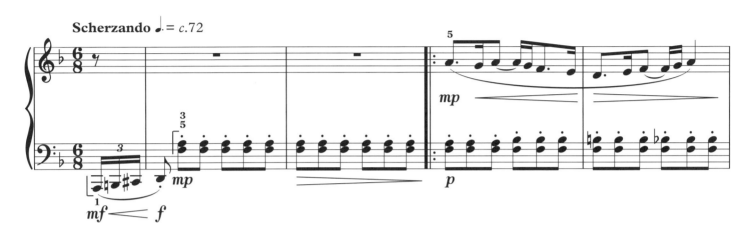

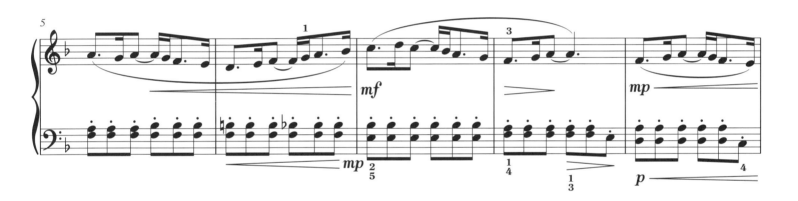

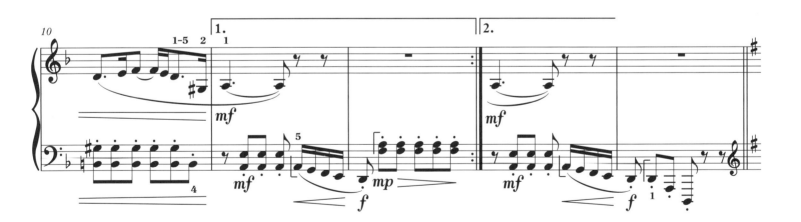

The Japanese composer Karen Tanaka studied composition and piano at the Tōhō Gakuen School of Music in Tokyo. She moved to Paris in 1986, working at Pierre Boulez's research institute IRCAM. Later, she studied with Luciano Berio in Florence (1990–1). She has taught in several American universities, and now lives in Los Angeles, teaching composition at the California Institute of the Arts. Her love of nature and concern for the environment are reflected in many of her compositions. The composer has written: 'Imagine a magical masquerade ball at the Carnival of Venice. Bars 13–31 should be played very lightly, like a fanciful and flirting butterfly.'

© 2016 by The Associated Board of the Royal Schools of Music

Reproduced from *Spectrum 5: 15 contemporary pieces for solo piano*, compiled by Thalia Myers (ABRSM)

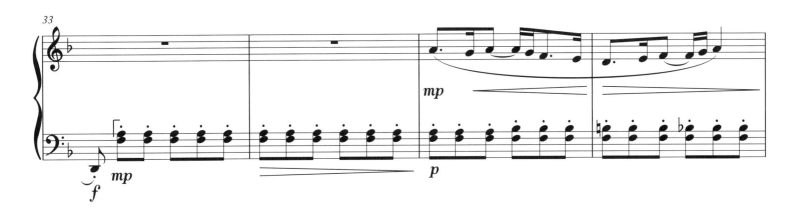

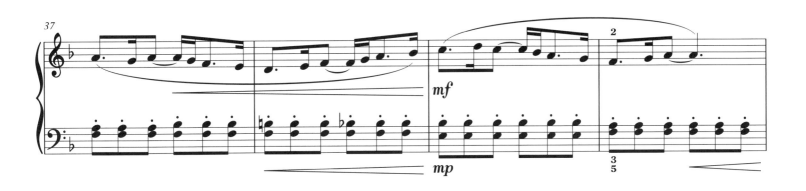

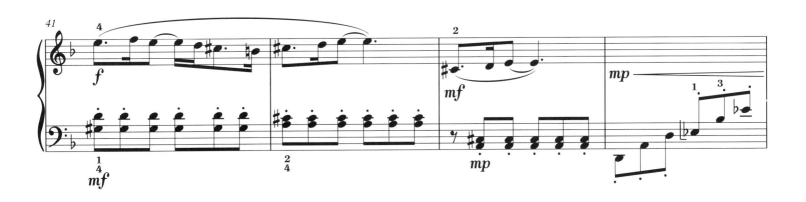